A TEACHER'S GUIDE TO UNDERSTANDING THE END TIMES

SAMUEL M. POWELL

D1343006

BEACON HILL PRESS
OF KANSAS CITY

Copyright 2011 by Samuel M. Powell and
Beacon Hill Press of Kansas City

ISBN 978-0-8341-2561-2

Printed in the
United States of America

Cover Design: Doug Bennett
Interior Design: Sharon Page

Library of Congress Cataloging-in-Publication Data

Powell, Samuel M.
   A teacher's guide to understanding the end times / Samuel M.
Powell.
        p. cm.
   Includes bibliographical references.
   ISBN 978-0-8341-2561-2 (pbk.)
   1. Eschatology—Study and teaching. I. Title.
   BT821.3.P67 2011
   236'.9—dc22

                                            2010052028

10 9 8 7 6 5 4 3 2 1

CONTENTS

PREFACE

As a member of a church with a Wesleyan heritage, I have studied our article of faith on resurrection, judgment, and the return of Christ. Our statement is brief and thoroughly traditional; it fits within the broad framework of historic Christian belief. Being comfortable with my church's statement, I'm puzzled by the popularity of speculative end-times theology. As a Wesleyan, I see little in this theology that resonates with the concerns of my tradition. On the contrary, the preachers of end-times theology seem to be operating with a very different agenda.

I've written this book in hopes that it can bring some clarity to these issues. In a subject known for its obscurity, clarity can be a good thing. Above all, my hope is that this book will offer some fresh perspectives as we all try to faithfully interpret the Bible.

1

WHAT'S UP WITH THE END TIMES?

If films are any indication, today's culture is fascinated with the idea of apocalyptic disaster. Nearly every summer Hollywood churns out a would-be blockbuster or two that portray cataclysmic destruction and speculate on the fate of the survivors. The plot is often predictable: life is going on as usual when something ominous happens. Then disaster strikes; millions of dollars of computer graphics and special effects appear on screen, depicting death, destruction, and doom. Attention next shifts to the survivors as they struggle to exist and overcome the threat. Finally, human ingenuity or luck eliminates the threat, and humankind turns to the task of rebuilding. Recently, speculation has focused on the Mayan calendar and its supposed prediction of worldwide mayhem in 2012. Predictably, in 2009 Hollywood released the film *2012* to capitalize on this sudden interest in calendars.

The formula for apocalyptic movies is so fixed (and successful) that about the only thing that changes is the threat. Is it aliens from outer space (as in *Independence Day* and *War of the Worlds*)? Or is it the effects of climate change (*Waterworld*, *The Day After Tomorrow*)?

Is it a biological plague (*I Am Legend*)? Is it nuclear holocaust (the *Terminator* movies)? Occasionally the disaster is narrowly avoided (as in *Armageddon*, in which fast action averts earth's destruction), but the point is always the same: We face a danger that threatens all human life—how will we respond?

Interest in apocalyptic matters is not limited to film. A recent twist on this theme asks the question, "What would the world be like if humans did not survive apocalyptic disaster?" This is the premise of the current television series *Life after People*. It explores how the natural world would reclaim cities and other human places once we are gone. Although this series doesn't focus on the sorts of catastrophes that might wipe out humanity, it still testifies to the interest people have in widespread destruction and possible annihilation.

The level of interest is confirmed by public opinion polls. In a poll conducted by Harris Interactive in 2002, 59 percent of Americans polled believed that "the events described in the Book of Revelation will occur at some point in the future," and 35 percent said that they "are paying more attention to how news events might relate to the end of the world."[1] Interest in the end, then, is widespread, even in the non-Christian population.

Clearly if we are looking for evidence of intense interest in the end times, we need look no further than the *Left Behind* series. Previous generations of Christians had their share of end-times media, including the 1970s film *A Thief in the Night* and Hal Lindsey's books. However, these media are only a trickle compared to the tsunami of the *Left Behind* books, films, and video games. The books have sold tens of millions of copies and been translated into numerous languages. These publications have transcended the boundaries of the Christian world and become a cultural phenomenon.

To be fair, not all Christians are fans of the *Left Behind* view of life. The Lutheran Church–Missouri Synod has offered this critique:

> In *Left Behind* trusting God for the future is often overshadowed and outweighed by a curiosity to know the details of that future. . . . [This series] causes more confusion when it promotes the idea that there is not just one return of Christ (the rapture), nor two (Christ's appearing to usher in his 1000-year rule), but three comings of Christ. The last advent, it teaches, will be at the end of the millennial reign or the Great White Throne Judgment of Rev 20:11–15.[2]

According to the organization Methodist Evangelicals Together,

> The idea that there will be two future comings of Jesus—one secret and one public—runs contrary to the plain teaching of Jesus and Paul. Passages such as 2 Thessalonians 1:5-10 and Matthew 24:36-44 show clearly that Jesus' coming to gather his people into his presence and his coming to judge the world belong to a single event.[3]

Unfortunately for the Lutherans and Evangelical Methodists, no one is listening to them. This is partly because, like the fascination with apocalyptic films, many people are deeply interested in colorful and speculative end-times subjects. Cautious Scripture-based teaching about the return of Jesus has a less sensational feel than the imaginative storytelling of apocalyptic movies and the *Left Behind* books. We've been trained by Hollywood and other media sources to desire vivid storylines and emotionally laden images. In comparison, traditional views of the end times seem unstimulating and flat.

So how should Christians think about apocalyptic matters? How should we interpret the Bible's texts that relate to the future? How can we navigate among the many opinions found in the Christian community? What is truly important in the Bible's teaching about the future?

To answer these questions, we must first lay some significant historical groundwork.

HISTORY OF CHRISTIAN ESCHATOLOGY

Our pursuit for answers commences with a brief look at the history of Christian eschatology. The term "eschatology" refers to subjects surrounding the end times, such as judgment, resurrection, and the return of Jesus. So we will begin with a look at eschatology—or end-times beliefs—in the Old and New Testaments and continue through the centuries to the status of eschatology today.

2

ESCHATOLOGY IN THE OLD TESTAMENT

Readers of the Old Testament are often surprised and disappointed to learn it contains only a modest eschatology. It has no real concept of life after death or resurrection (except for Dan. 12:2). Similarly, it has no belief in a future judgment and rewards and punishments for individuals. Instead, all the emphasis falls on the restoration of Israel as a nation. Isaiah's words give us a good example of Old Testament eschatology.

Isaiah looked forward to "the day of the LORD" (see 13:6, 9), which would be a day of judgment and destruction on Israel and the other nations. Beyond this destruction, Isaiah believed that God would raise a future king who would be like David and would rule with wisdom and justice (11:1-5). His rule would coincide with a time of peace (11:6-8; 60:18) and with divine blessing, as God would provide a universal banquet and remove all pain and sorrow (25:6-8). In the meantime, Jerusalem would be restored and become the center of the world. The nations would flock to Jerusalem to learn God's law (2:2-4), and their wealth would beautify the temple (60:13). Israel would be filled with righteousness and people would enjoy full life spans without fear and worry (65:17-25).

Isaiah's eschatology, with its focus on Israel's restoration, is typical of Old Testament eschatology: after the exile in Babylon, Jerusalem and the temple will be rebuilt. Israel will for once have a good and righteous king who will enforce justice in the land. Israel's enemies will be destroyed once and for all. The other nations will come to Jerusalem to worship Israel's God. The land of Israel will be blessed and produce enough food to support the nation. Peace and prosperity will abound. Everyone will live to a good, old age before dying.

3

APOCALYPTICISM

In the newest parts of the Old Testament (such as Zech. 9–12) and in later Jewish literature we find the development of a new eschatology, one that differs significantly from Isaiah's eschatology. This new eschatology was apocalypticism. The term "apocalypticism" is based on the Greek word for revelation. An apocalypse is a revelation. Apocalypticism is so called because this literature often presents itself as being the result of direct revelation from God.

How does apocalyptic eschatology differ from earlier eschatology? For one thing, apocalypticism affirms belief in the judgment and resurrection of individuals. Previously the emphasis fell on the nation of Israel. In apocalypticism, however, there is the belief that individuals will face God's judgment, will be raised from the dead, and will receive reward or punishment. For another thing, apocalyptic literature draws a firm distinction between this present age and the age to come. In most of the Old Testament, the day of the Lord is simply that moment in history when God finally and decisively acts on Israel's behalf, bringing judgment and salvation. The present age has plenty of sin, but it's not hopeless. God is still at work in the world. In apocalyptic thought, however, the present age is portrayed in completely bleak terms. It is seen as given over to the powers of sin and evil. God, seemingly, is not at work; on the contrary, the present age is characterized mainly by its persecution of God's people. As a result, there is no sense that the present age can be redeemed. Hope is concerned only with the age to come.

There are other characteristics of apocalypticism. It tends to divide humanity into two groups: the children of light and the children of darkness. There is no moral ambiguity in humanity. Everyone is on the side of either God or evil. Those who are evil belong to this present age, which is likewise under the control of evil spiritual powers.

Apocalyptic literature also has a distinctive view of history. Not only does it sharply distinguish the present age from the age to come, but it also often describes the present age as consisting in a series of ages, each ruled by a great world empire (as in Dan. 7). History is thus seen as having a fixed course. Each age follows the previous age according to a fixed schedule. The final age, with the last empire, will be characterized by violence against God's people and the near destruction of Jerusalem. The kingdom of God follows the final age and brings history to a close by destroying the final empire and saving Israel.

In the apocalyptic understanding of reality, then, the present age is filled with evil and God's people are threatened. There is no hope except for an act of God that will radically eliminate evil and restore Israel. Things are bad now and will get a lot worse before the end. Shortly before the end, both society and nature will be thrown into terrible distress. Then, in a cata-

clysmic event, God will go to war with the powers of
evil and destroy them.

As mentioned, there is some apocalyptic literature in the Old Testament. But more of this literature
flourished in the two centuries before Jesus—at a time
when Israel was under great stress from foreign nations.
During this time, the apocalyptic message sustained
the faith of devout Jews by promising them that their
sufferings were temporary and that any who died as
martyrs would be resurrected and given eternal life.

The apocalyptic spirit was alive and well in the
time of Jesus. There was, it seems, a large community
devoted to apocalyptic beliefs. One of the products of
this community was John the Baptist. Although we do
not know all of John's beliefs, his message (as portrayed
in the Gospels—see Matt. 3; Mark 1; Luke 3; and John
1) fits with the apocalyptic framework: the kingdom
of God is near; therefore, Israel must repent. Jewish
status is not enough; Jews must produce obedience and
good works. Soon, the promised One will come and
introduce a baptism of fire, that is, of judgment.

4

ESCHATOLOGY IN THE
NEW TESTAMENT

The New Testament stands within the tradition of Jewish apocalyptic thinking. Almost every book of the New Testament expresses some important aspect of apocalypticism.

The Gospels portray Jesus' message in apocalyptic terms. He came preaching the nearness of the kingdom of God. His acts of healing, feeding, and casting out demons demonstrated the power of the kingdom pushing against the power of Satan. He expressly taught apocalyptic beliefs—persecution of God's people before the end (Matt. 24:9; Mark 13:9); the end-time woes and suffering (Matt. 24:21); the coming, decisive end of the present age (v. 3); the violence against Jerusalem (Luke 21:20-24); judgment, reward, and punishment for all individuals (Matt. 25:31-46); and God's direct intervention. John's gospel likewise breathes in the atmosphere of apocalypticism. We can see this in its sharp contrast between the community of disciples, who walk in the light, and the world, which abides in darkness. The Gospels, then, are apocalyptic in character. They see the present age as controlled by Satan. They portray Jesus' ministry as God's kingdom invading Satan's domain. And they see history as marching toward a preordained, catastrophic end, culminating in the new age of God's kingdom.

At the same time, the gospel writers were concerned to temper their readers' apocalyptic expectations. This is especially so for Luke. For instance, Luke narrated a parable about a rich man who went on a long journey and whose slaves had no idea when he would return. Luke prefaced this parable with the comment that Jesus told the parable "because they supposed that the kingdom of God was to appear immediately" (19:11). This was Luke's way of warning his readers that nobody could know when Jesus would return and that even in Jesus' day people were mistakenly speculating about his return. Luke also included in his gospel a story in which a Pharisee asked Jesus "when the kingdom of God was coming." To this question Jesus replied that "the kingdom of God is not coming with things that can be observed" (17:20). Again, this is Luke's way of warning his readers not to be preoccupied with signs and with the attempt to infer the coming of the kingdom from signs. Finally, Luke began the book of Acts with the disciples asking the same question that the Pharisee asked: "Lord, is this the time when you will restore the kingdom to Israel?" In response Jesus stated, "It is not for you to know the times or periods that the Father has set" (1:6-7). Luke's inclusion of this story is once again a message for his readers: Disciples are to be at work for God's kingdom. They should not waste time wondering about the end of this age.

Paul's theology likewise travels within an apocalyptic landscape. The main apocalyptic event for Paul was Christ's resurrection, which was the "first fruits" of the general resurrection (1 Cor. 15:23), and which signals that the end of this age has arrived (10:11). As a result,

Paul believed that the return of Christ was near (Rom. 13:12; 1 Cor. 7:26, 29, 31). Paul's congregations shared his expectation. The Thessalonians thought that Jesus' return was so near that they panicked when a few in the congregation died; they thought they would all still be living by the time Jesus returned. Paul also saw the world as (in some sense) controlled by evil powers (1 Cor. 2:6, 8; Rom. 8:38), although he was confident that their time was limited (1 Cor. 2:6).

Finally, let's consider the book of Revelation. First, its title—in Greek, *Apocalypsis*—tells us immediately that it stands within the apocalyptic tradition. Additionally, the book abounds in apocalyptic themes, such as judgment for individuals, rewards and punishments, end-time persecution of God's people, calamities in society and nature, and the eventual destruction of God's enemies.

In summary, the New Testament exhibits all the features of apocalypticism. Early Christians had a firm belief in the apocalyptic message and many (perhaps most) believed the return of Jesus was near (Rev. 1:1-3; 22:6, 12, 20). They saw the resurrection of Jesus as the first in a series of events that would usher in the end of this age and the beginning of God's kingdom. Christianity, then, from its beginning was nourished on apocalyptic hopes.

5

ESCHATOLOGY AFTER
THE NEW TESTAMENT

The New Testament's apocalypticism passed over into the belief of second- and third-century Christians. Major writers of these centuries all testify to a belief that Jesus would return soon and establish the thousand-year kingdom mentioned in Rev. 20. Clearly we don't know what every Christian believed about these matters; only a handful bothered to write anything that has survived. Further, the church as a whole did not issue any statements on eschatology—there are no official creeds from the second and third centuries. Nonetheless, the writings we do possess indicate that apocalyptic beliefs were the norm in these centuries.

However, disagreement lay on the horizon. Some Christians (perhaps most) believed in a literal thousand-year earthly reign of Jesus at the end of this age. They also held to a rather literal fulfillment of Old Testament prophecies about Israel. They thus believed that in the resurrected state humans would live on earth in material bodies, eating and drinking, and that the nations would literally bring their wealth to Jerusalem. Belief in a literal thousand-year rule of Christ came to be called chiliasm (from the Greek word for "thousand"). The thousand-year rule is often referred to as the *millennium* (Latin for "thousand years").

As time went on, however, more and more people within the church began to interpret these prophetic passages, and especially the idea of the millennium, in spiritual or symbolic terms. The millennium was thus regarded as a symbol of God's triumph over sin but not as a literal rule on the earth. In AD 381 the church issued a statement formally opposing chiliasm. In the creed written by the Council of Constantinople (commonly referred to as the Nicene Creed), the church affirmed that Christ's kingdom would have no end. This assertion denied the idea of a literal millennium, which seemed to suggest that Christ's kingdom would have an end after a thousand years. Although chiliasm continued to find some support in the Christian community, it was increasingly a minority view.

Christian eschatology was for the next fifteen hundred years in much of Europe shaped by the thought of Augustine (354–430), a bishop in North Africa (modern-day Tunisia). Augustine introduced a new way of thinking about the millennium. It began, he believed, with the first appearance of Christ and would end with Christ's return at the end of this age. The millennial reign of Christ was simply the age of the church. Christ was ruling in and through the church. Augustine thus clearly denied a literal rule of Christ on earth. For many Christians in Europe, Augustine's view was convincing.

From the 200s to the 1700s many Christians relied on biblical prophecy, especially Daniel and Revelation, to understand their times. They believed these biblical books outlined major events in world history. This sort of interpretation was especially common during the

Reformation (1500s–1600s), when Protestants used the prophetic books to interpret their struggles with the Catholic Church. Some Protestants thus saw the pope as the Antichrist. The Muslim Turkish Empire was seen to be the Gog and Magog of Ezekiel (see 38–39). And times of social stress brought forth renewed hopes for the return of Christ, as in the English civil war of the 1640s.

6

ESCHATOLOGY IN THE NINETEENTH CENTURY

The nineteenth century represents a turning point in Christian eschatology and the return of chiliasm. Throughout the nineteenth century, two eschatologies competed with each other. One saw the millennium as the result of the progressive Christianizing of the world; the other saw the millennium as God's radical intervention into a world of sin and evil. The first saw human history advancing progressively toward the millennium; the second saw history becoming more and more evil until the coming of the kingdom.

Revivalistic Eschatology

The first eschatology, with the optimistic view of history, was developed in response to the Great Awakening. This was a widespread revival movement of the 1700s in America, a movement that saw many dramatic conversions and had an enormous impact on the church. From the experience of this great revival the America theologian Jonathon Edwards (1703-58) came to believe that the Awakening was the beginning of a worldwide revival and that Christ's millennial kingdom would begin when the entire world had been evangelized. For Edwards, human history was moving in a positive direction. The millennium would be the culmination of the Awakening.

Throughout the nineteenth century, Edwards's view proved persuasive for many Christians, especially those with close connections to revivalism. Alexander Campbell (1788–1866) sought to overcome disunity among denominations by returning to the beliefs and practices of the New Testament church (as he understood them). He believed that by restoring early Christianity he was preparing the way for the millennium. Charles Finney (1792–1875), a noted revivalist, felt that the great revivals and social reforms of the nineteenth century were preparing the world for Christ's kingdom. In his view, the church's task was to transform the world through holding revivals and eliminating social evils. Once this transformation had taken place and the entire world had seen revival, Christ would return and establish his kingdom on earth. Finney seemed to believe that this transformation could be accomplished within a few years. The nineteenth-century Holiness Movement agreed with Finney's eschatology and optimistically threw itself into social reform and revivalism.

The main thing to keep in mind about this kind of eschatology is its view that what happens in history contributes positively to Christ's coming. For theologians with this outlook, revivalism and social reform make the world better and thus make the world fit for Christ to return. The millennial rule of Christ brings this work of revival and reform to completion. Accordingly, this eschatology encouraged Christians to be hopeful, not only about Christ's return but also about their efforts. As they held revivals and engaged in social reform, they believed they were contributing directly to changes that would usher in Christ's kingdom on earth.

Speculative Apocalyptic Eschatology

The second kind of eschatology found in the nineteenth century represented a return to apocalyptic themes. It's difficult to locate the beginning of this eschatology, but one important representative was the Scottish pastor Edward Irving (1792–1834). Irving's eschatology took the book of Revelation quite literally. He thus believed that the church had largely fallen away from God, that Jews would be restored to the land of Israel, and that Christ's return was imminent. Irving's view would come to have a big impact on later theologians.

In the meantime, apocalyptic expectations were heating up in America. A pastor, William Miller (1782–1849), had come to believe he had unlocked the secret of Christ's return. For Miller, the key was a correct understanding of Dan. 8:14, which prophesies that "the sanctuary shall be restored" after 2,300 days. He interpreted the restoration of the sanctuary to mean the return of Christ and the general resurrection; he criticized those who believed that Daniel was talking about a literal temple. Miller also believed that biblical writers often spoke of "days" when they meant "years" prophetically. The 2,300 days of Dan. 8:14 thus represented 2,300 years. He held that the 2,300 years began in 457 BC when (he believed) a decree was issued to rebuild the temple that had been destroyed by the Babylonians in the previous century. Adding 2,300 years to 457 BC yielded the date AD 1843 as the expected year of Christ's return.

Miller then turned his attention to the other important numbers in Daniel, the 1,290 and 1,335 days of Dan. 12:11-12. Through a complex calculation, Miller decided these figures described epochs of European history. In particular, they pointed to the rise of the Catholic Church and its domination of the church. Miller believed that the 1,290 "days" (i.e., years) ended in 1798, when the Catholic Church in France was deprived of its power during the French Revolution. Miller's calculations reinforced his earlier conclusion that the return of Jesus would take place in 1843, 45 years after 1798 (1,335 - 1,290 = 45). So the 1,335 "days" of Daniel represent the time between the rise of the Catholic Church and the return of Christ. Miller eventually softened his calculation and believed that Christ might come as late as 1844.

There had been attempts at calculating the return of Christ before Miller; however, no one before him applied himself so diligently to the task. And certainly no one before Miller had the effect he had. Thousands became convinced by his teaching and prepared themselves for Christ's return in 1843 or 1844. Sadly for Miller, Christ did not return as predicted. This event was so traumatic to his followers that it has been dubbed the Great Disappointment.

Many followers gave up hope or at least the obsession with date setting. But the human spirit is resilient. Some followers believed Miller had been mostly right. In particular, they agreed that his calculation of dates had been correct. Help came when one of Miller's followers, Hiram Edson (1808-82), had a vision of Christ moving into the holiest part of the heavenly sanctuary.

From this vision came the view that Miller had misunderstood what was to happen in 1843-44. For Edson and others (who would eventually form the Seventh-Day Adventist Church), 1843-44 signaled, not the end of this age, but instead Christ's transfer from one part of the heavenly temple to another. So Miller had been right on the dates but wrong on their significance. Something momentous had occurred, but it was not the end—just the prelude to the end. What, then, was Christ doing in the holiest part of the temple? He was thought to be conducting the first phase of God's judgment (the "investigative judgment"). Thus 1843-44 held great significance for eschatology.

Back in Ireland, a pastor named John Nelson Darby (1800-1882) was developing a distinctive eschatology. Darby was, to some extent, influenced by Irving's theology. However, he introduced some important innovations. The most important was the idea of dispensations. Darby came to believe that human history was divided into eras ("dispensations"). Each was characterized by a specific way in which God related to humankind. For eschatology, the most important dispensations were the eras of law and grace. The era of law encompassed the period from the giving of the law until the final fulfillment of God's promises to Israel. The dispensation of grace covered the church age.

This idea of dispensations meant there was an important and abiding difference between the church and Israel. Prior to Darby, the church had taught that it was the new Israel—that divine promises made to Israel had been or would be fulfilled in the church. The church was thus the center of God's activity in

the world. For Darby, however, promises made to Israel
were not fulfilled in the church. On the contrary, Israel
and the church had different destinies. The church's
destiny was heavenly; Israel's was earthly. Old Testament prophecies that related to Israel, therefore, spoke
only about earthly realities and not about the church's
heavenly destiny. This sharp distinction between Israel
and the church meant that, for Darby, the church age
was a sort of interruption in the dispensation with Israel. Israel, in this case, was the main focus of God's
activity in the world. The church age was a detour.
God's plans demanded that the church be removed so
that God's work with Israel could be resumed. We can
see that Darby's theology departed significantly from
traditional Christian eschatology. Even in the second
and third centuries, when many Christians believed in
a literal millennium, no one in the church envisioned
the restoration of Israel. Christians uniformly saw the
church, not Israel, as the fulfillment of Old Testament
prophecies.

The need to get the church out of the way led to
Darby's idea of the secret rapture of the church—the
idea that Christ would miraculously transfer all Christians to heaven. Prior to Darby, the church had taught
that Jesus comes to the earth twice: first as the humble man from Nazareth, then as the glorious Lord and
Judge. However, Darby's theory of the church required
him to believe that Jesus would come an additional
time—seven years prior to the final coming—to pull
the church out of the world. This point needs some
explanation. Darby believed that as a sign of the end
times, the church of his day had largely fallen away

from God. This evaluation stemmed from his view that every dispensation ends in failure. His theology thus required him to believe that the church age was doomed to failure and that nothing could revive the church. The rapture was thus the removal of only a small part of the church—the faithful remnant.

Following the rapture, according to Darby, would be a time of tribulation. During this time, many Jews would support the Antichrist; some however (the remnant of faithful, law-observing Jews) would not and would be persecuted. After the tribulation Jesus would return a third time and introduce his millennial rule.

Because, for Darby, Old Testament promises and prophecies pertained to Israel and not the church, it was necessary for the Jews to be restored to the land of Israel. Darby thus reconnected with the tradition of biblical apocalypticism. He shared the ancient Jewish apocalyptic hope that Israel would be restored and all the prophecies literally fulfilled in the Jewish people.

Since (according to Darby) the dispensation of the church was (like all the others) doomed to end in human failure and disobedience, Darby rejected the revivalistic, optimistic eschatology of Edwards, Finney, and others. For him it was just impossible to imagine the gospel sweeping across the world and preparing for Christ's return through the work of the church. On the contrary, he believed history was moving in a negative direction. Evil was increasing and would increase until the third coming of Jesus and his kingdom.

Darby was instrumental in founding the denomination known as the Plymouth Brethren. He went on to exert an influence in America, to which he trav-

eled several times in the 1860s and 1870s on speaking tours. In fact, so great was his influence that many
evangelical Christians adopted his eschatology. While
in the mid-nineteenth century most evangelicals such
as Finney and those in the Holiness Movement held to
the revivalistic, optimistic eschatology, by the beginning of the twentieth century many and perhaps most
evangelicals affirmed Darby's apocalyptic eschatology,
with its ideas of dispensations and the secret rapture.
It is thus appropriate to speak of dispensationalism as a
distinct theological movement.

One step in dispensationalism's growing success
was the series of meetings known as the Niagara Bible Conference (which began in 1868 and then met
in Niagara, Ontario, from 1883 to 1897). Although
these meetings had a general focus on prophecy, they
quickly became dominated by the dispensationalist
perspective. The 1878 meeting adopted a creed. Article fourteen of that creed was a clear statement of dispensationalist theology. It expressly denied that there
would be a worldwide revival (contrary to Finney). It
affirmed that the church would mostly fall away from
God and that the Jews would be restored to the land
of Israel. The importance of the Niagara meetings for
eschatology was twofold: (1) They brought together
leaders of American evangelicalism, and (2) they cre-
ated an evangelical consensus about dispensationalism.
The Niagara meetings were important for another reason: they contributed directly and substantially to the
movement known as fundamentalism. The theology of
fundamentalism was essentially the theology of the Niagara Bible Conference; as a result, people who believe

in the rapture are often fundamentalists or heavily influenced by fundamentalism.

The influence of dispensationalism also spread through other means. One was the publication of the *Scofield Study Bible* (first published in 1909). This edition of the Bible contained notes by Cyrus I. Scofield (1843–1921) that were expressly dispensationalist. Through this study Bible dispensationalist ideas gained widespread popularity among conservative Christians in America. Dispensationalism additionally increased its impact by finding a home in several educational institutions, especially Dallas Theological Seminary and Moody Bible Institute.[4]

7

ESCHATOLOGY TODAY

Christian eschatology has come a long way since the New Testament. What is its status today?

For many churches, little has changed since the nineteenth century. Most denominations have articles of faith on eschatological topics. These articles are almost always brief. Here, for instance, is what the Church of the Nazarene says about eschatological matters:

> We believe that the Lord Jesus Christ will come again; that we who are alive at His coming shall not precede them that are asleep in Christ Jesus; but that, if we are abiding in Him, we shall be caught up with the risen saints to meet the Lord in the air, so that we shall ever be with the Lord. . . .
>
> . . . We believe in the resurrection of the dead, that the bodies both of the just and of the unjust shall be raised to life and united with their spirits—"they that have done good, unto the resurrection of life; and they that have done evil, unto the resurrection of damnation."
>
> . . . We believe in future judgment in which every person shall appear before God to be judged according to his or her deeds in this life.

. . . We believe that glorious and everlasting life is assured to all who savingly believe in, and obediently follow, Jesus Christ our Lord; and that the finally impenitent shall suffer eternally in hell.[5]

What is notable about this statement is its use of biblical language. The first paragraph is essentially a paraphrase of 1 Thess. 4:15-17. The second paragraph similarly brings together affirmations from various places in the Bible.

This statement is also notable for what it does not say. It does not mention the millennium, the tribulation, and the secret rapture of the church. It says nothing about a secret coming of Jesus prior to the tribulation. In fact, it really takes no stand on any other controversial topics that arose in the nineteenth century. This statement was written with great care in such a way as to avoid associating the denomination with dispensationalism and fundamentalism. It locates its members firmly within the mainstream of Christian thinking about eschatology by focusing on central and historic affirmations.

Other responsible and careful statements of faith (including those of the Southern Baptist Convention, the Presbyterian Church USA, the Free Methodist Church, and the Wesleyan Church) are similar to the Nazarene statement. In each case we find carefully worded affirmations that express the historic faith of the Christian church and avoid speculative ideas about the end times.

At the same time, dispensationalism is alive and well. Some denominations have used dispensationalist concepts in their articles of faith. The Assemblies of

God, for example, affirms that "the second coming of Christ includes the rapture of the saints, which is our blessed hope, followed by the visible return of Christ with His saints to reign on earth for one thousand years. This millennial reign will bring the salvation of national Israel, and the establishment of universal peace."[6] We see here the familiar concerns of dispensationalism: the rapture, the millennium, and the role of Israel in the end times. Calvary Chapel congregations and many popular speakers likewise affirm dispensational views.

Despite some similarities between eschatology today and in the nineteenth century, there is an important difference. It's a difference we have mentioned earlier. In the nineteenth century, the mainstream of evangelical Christianity endorsed the revivalistic eschatology of Jonathon Edwards and Charles Finney; in the twentieth century evangelicals adopted the speculative apocalyptic eschatology of dispensationalism. Today, in the twenty-first century, this dispensationalist trend continues. It's a trend that has also gone hand in hand with the rise of the nondenominational movement. The theology of independent churches and parachurch ministries are typically dispensationalist. As increasing numbers have left denominations and joined nondenominational churches, the number of American Christians with dispensationalist views has increased. A recent (2006) opinion poll found that 33 percent of Christians believe "the specific timing of Christ's return to earth is revealed in biblical prophecies" and that 34 percent believe "this will occur after the world situation worsens and reaches a low point"—a traditional feature of apocalyptic eschatology. Further, a majority of evangelicals believe that "God gave [the state of] Israel to the Jewish people" (69 percent) and "that [the state of] Israel is the fulfillment of biblical prophecy" (59 percent).[7] Dispensationalist ideas, then, have become widespread. Let's have a closer look at dispensationalism today.

8

DISPENSATIONAL THEOLOGY TODAY

Contemporary dispensational theology is, above all, a way of interpreting the Bible. (In theology, we use the term "hermeneutic" to refer to "a method or principle of interpretation."[8] Dispensationalism thus has a distinctive hermeneutic.) First, it continues to assume that when the book of Daniel refers to days or weeks, it really means years. Additionally, contemporary dispensationalists believe strongly in what they call "literal" interpretation. What they mean is that Old Testament prophecies that predict a restoration of Israel actually do relate to historical Israel in the future. The prophecies do not relate to the church. As a result, dispensationalists have interpreted the creation of the state of Israel as a direct fulfillment of biblical prophecy.

Moreover, since some eschatological passages in the Bible (notably Dan. 9:27 and 11:31; Matt. 24:15; 2 Thess. 2:4; and Rev. 11:1-2) refer to the temple, dispensationalists believe that it will be rebuilt and that sacrifices will resume. Because the purification rituals of the temple require (among other things) the ashes of a red heifer, there is today considerable activity on the Internet speculating about and reporting on the search for a red heifer. At least one American cattle breeder has contacted some rabbis in Jerusalem about helping them obtain one.[9]

Dispensationalists, following the book of Daniel and other biblical books, also believe that once the church is raptured to heaven, Israel will become the center of world history. At some point during the tribulation, Israel will be attacked by the Antichrist and nearly destroyed before being rescued by Jesus at his second (actually, third) coming. For dispensationalists, all this is implied by a literal reading of biblical prophecy.

The result of this interest in Israel has been the rise of Christian Zionism. Christian Zionists believe the land occupied by ancient Israel has always belonged to the Jews and belongs to them today. They regard Palestinians as squatters who have stolen the Jews' land, and they wholeheartedly support the state of Israel's harsh treatment of the Palestinians. Christian Zionists give their support because they believe dispensationalist theories can only work if Israel retains control of its land and gains complete control over Jerusalem. That is, the fulfillment of biblical prophecies requires that Israel control the land it occupies. What comes from this way of thinking is an odd situation that finds many American evangelicals giving unquestionable support to Israel's policies, no matter what they may involve.

Another aspect of contemporary dispensationalist theology is the belief that the church has, for the most part, fallen away from God. They refer to this as the great apostasy. On the basis of 2 Thess. 2:3 ("that day will not come unless the rebellion comes first. . . .") dispensationalists generally believe that since we are living in the end times, the church must have fallen away. And as they look around at the church world, they find plenty they don't like that confirms their view. As they

see it, whole branches of the church such as the Ortho-
dox churches, the Roman Catholic Church, the Angli-
can churches, and many American denominations are
simply not part of the Christian world.

Dispensationalist thinking additionally includes
a distrust of government. Although dispensationalists trust Israel's government, they are extremely sus-
picious of other governments. But what really makes
them anxious is the thought of a worldwide government—hence their anger toward the United Nations
(which takes a dim view of Israel's treatment of the
Palestinians). The anxiety of dispensationalists is root-
ed in the idea that during the tribulation the world will
come under the domination of a single power, the Antichrist. This fear is driven in part by their interpretation
of Dan. 7, which describes a succession of four world
empires, represented as wild beasts. Dispensationalists
typically associate the fourth beast of Daniel with the
Roman Empire. But since the Roman Empire ceased
to exist centuries ago, dispensationalists believe it (or
a modern version of it) will be reconstituted and serve
as the basis of the Antichrist's power. Dispensationalists routinely hold that the European Union (originally
called the Common Market) is the forerunner of the
revived Roman Empire. Again, however, there is a her-
meneutical problem, for in Daniel's vision the fourth
beast has ten horns, symbolizing kings. It's proven difficult for dispensationalists to correlate the idea of ten
kings with the twenty-seven member nations of the
European Union.

Dispensationalists are also noted for their belief
that the return of Jesus is near. They have to be careful

on this point, since Jesus said that not even the Son of Man knows the hour or day of his return (e.g., Matt. 24:36). Nonetheless, a review of dispensationalist literature shows an elevated confidence that the rapture will be occurring very soon. This confidence is based on a reading of signs. For dispensationalists, recent history has provided clear and unmistakable signs that the end of this age is near. The creation of the state of Israel is the chief sign; however, there are others. One popular end-times writer observes that recent astronomical discoveries of planets outside our solar system fulfills the prophecy that "there will be signs in the sun, the moon, and the stars" (Luke 21:25).[10] Others frequently point to the high incidence of war, famine, and other disasters as signs that the return of Jesus is near.

INTERPRETING
THE BIBLE

We've spent a lot of time so far reviewing the development of Christian eschatology. Some readers may find the history tedious, but the history helps us see that biblical interpretation is no easy matter, especially when it comes to eschatology. The history of Christian eschatology shows us that Christians have had differing opinions and have interpreted the Bible is various ways.

However, the diversity of opinions does not mean faithful, responsible interpretation is impossible; all it really requires is a proper orientation to the Bible. So let's look at a few things that will help us approach and read the Bible in an appropriate way.

9

THE BIBLE'S PURPOSE

Responsible interpretation of the Bible pays attention to the Bible's purpose; it is a way of honoring that purpose. This purpose is stated clearly in 2 Tim. 3:16-17:

All scripture is inspired by God and is useful for teaching, for reproof, for correction, and for training in righteousness, so that everyone who belongs to God may be proficient, equipped for every good work.

The interpreter, then, must constantly keep in view the goal, which is "training in righteousness" and equipping God's people "for every good work."

Unfortunately, it cannot be said with assurance that speculative end-times theology honors the Bible's purpose. It is true that much of this theology presents itself as a ministry of warning. By trying to discern the signs of the times, it gives the appearance of helping Christians prepare for the end. For instance, here is a statement from Tim LaHaye's Web site:

Dr. LaHaye and PTRC [the Pre-Trib Research Center] stress three practical implications that flow from the rapture teaching. The first implication of pretribulationism is that it leads to godly living in an unholy age. Next, this New Testament teaching promotes a strong emphasis upon evangelism of the lost. Finally, when believers come to understand this eternal perspective, it leads to a zeal for worldwide missions.[11]

These goals seem praiseworthy. However, there is no evidence that end-times speculation promotes any of them. Endless guessing games about the identity of the Antichrist and bizarre interpretations of biblical symbols simply do not lead to more godly living or concern for the lost. Often these topics only lead to heated discussions.

In coming to terms with chiliasm many centuries ago, the church collectively decided that an emphasis on end-times speculation simply does not promote Christian living, which, as we've observed from 2 Timothy, is the purpose of the Bible. Instead, the mental gymnastics involved in end-times speculation only feeds curiosity. End-times speculation is popular for the same reason crossword puzzles, Sudoku, and mystery novels are popular. Humans love to figure things out. End-times theology presents people with a great puzzle and clues to solving the puzzle. As current events are interpreted using the clues, they are fitted together like jigsaw pieces so that a complete picture of the immediate future can gradually appear. The problem is that this puzzle approach to eschatology doesn't require faith; non-Christians can play this game just as well as Christians can. It doesn't increase godliness; there is no evidence that end-times puzzle solvers are better Christians.

All that end-times speculation really does is to scratch our itch for knowledge about the future. And it doesn't even do that very well. Christian history is filled with attempts to predict end-times events. Nearly every century has seen some movement convinced it held the key to understanding the end times. There is no reason to think that today's end-times specialists have any more insight than those of previous generations. The problem that all end-times theologians have is not a lack of insight or intelligence. The problem is that they interpret the Bible according to *their* purpose (which is to satisfy their curiosity) instead of interpreting according to the Bible's purpose. When we pay attention to the Bible's purpose—"training in righteousness"—we find that an intense interest in end-times matters is at best irrelevant. At worst, it may actually distract us from our true calling as Christian disciples.

10

THE MEANING OF BIBLICAL TEXTS

Dispensationalists and many other end-times thinkers insist biblical prophecies must be interpreted literally. This means they reject other methods of interpretation, such as the idealist and historicist approaches that will be described in chapter 11. For dispensationalists, literal interpretation means the prophecies must be fulfilled in Israel. Israel, as understood here, includes not only the Jewish people but also the land and national existence of Israel. Moreover these prophecies could not be fulfilled until Israel's national existence was restored, as was the case in 1948. Dispensationalists are committed to this literal method of interpretation.

Here is a clear statement about this method of interpretation:

"There is one, and only one, interpretation of any passage of scripture." And, dear friends, that is the bottom line in understanding any communication. And there is no more abused principle in the history of interpretation of the Word of God than the principle of the single sense. Whether by ignorance or design, great harm has been brought to the cause of Christ by the use of sensus plenior or multiple

senses. . . . the use of a dual hermeneutic which
applies the literal hermeneutic to the great majority
of Scripture and the spiritualizing hermeneutic to a
portion of prophecy, namely, that portion which is
future only and not even all of that, has its dangers.[12]

The problem with this view is that it is wrong. It is
simply incorrect to say that "there is one, and only one,
interpretation of any passage of scripture." Such a statement ignores the different interpretations a passage of
Scripture may have within the Bible itself.

Consider, for example, Matt. 2:15: "This was to
fulfill what had been spoken by the Lord through the
prophet, 'Out of Egypt I have called my son.'" This
verse is Matthew's commentary on Joseph, Mary, and
Jesus returning to Israel from Egypt. Matthew viewed
this return as the fulfillment of Hos. 11:1 ("When Israel was a child, I loved him, and out of Egypt I called
my son"). In Hosea, the words "out of Egypt I called
my son" refer to Israel's journey from Egypt in the exodus.
It is unreasonable to imagine that Hosea, while com-
posing these words, was thinking of Joseph, Mary, and
Jesus hundreds of years in his future. Yet Matthew sees
in Israel's journey from Egypt an anticipation of Jesus'
own journey. Jesus, in other words, reenacts Israel's
history—his life repeats Israel's history. So the words
"out of Egypt I called my son" have a double application. They refer (in Hosea) to Israel's experience in the
exodus. They also refer to Jesus as the One who repeats
Israel's history. The only way end-times theologians can
insist that each scripture has only one interpretation is
by ignoring the way New Testament writers actually
use the Old Testament.

As a second example, consider 1 Cor. 9:9-11: "It is written in the law of Moses, 'You shall not muzzle an ox while it is treading out the grain.' Is it for oxen that God is concerned? . . . It was indeed for our sake. . . . If we have sown spiritual good among you, is it too much if we reap your material benefits?" In 1 Corinthians, Paul was saying that ministers of the gospel have the right to be financially supported by their congregations (even though Paul did not insist on exercising this right). In support of his point, he drew on Deut. 25:4 ("You shall not muzzle an ox while it is treading out the grain"). If an ox is allowed to eat some of the grain it is treading, shouldn't ministers be able to derive material support from their ministerial work? Clearly in Deuteronomy this saying really is about oxen. It is a law that commands considerate treatment of animals as they work; it really is not about Christian ministers and their support. But Paul believed that this rule about oxen had an important application to his own situation. The point for us is that this saying about oxen, like Hos. 11:1, has a double application within the Bible. It speaks about oxen; but it can speak about Christian ministers as well. Once again we see the unreasonableness of insisting that every biblical passage has only one interpretation.

The lesson to learn from these examples is that New Testament writers were not concerned only with a literal interpretation of the Old Testament. On the contrary, there is a tradition within the Bible of finding new significance in Old Testament texts. The significance of a text in its original setting does not exhaust its interpretive possibilities. Think of 2 Cor. 4:6. Here

Paul referred to Gen. 1: "It is the God who said, 'Let light shine out of darkness,' who has shone in our hearts to give the light of the knowledge of the glory of God in the face of Jesus Christ." If Paul were concerned only with a literal interpretation of Gen. 1, he would have written only about the six days of creation. Instead, Paul saw that Gen. 1 had a significance that went beyond the creation of the world. For him, God's creation of light referred not only to physical light but also to the spiritual light that enables us to know Jesus Christ. New Testament writers routinely interpret the Old Testament in this way. For them, the Old Testament refers both to things in Israel's history and to things in the new covenant. It thus makes little sense for end-times theologians to claim that biblical passages have only a single interpretation. There is no good reason to assume that biblical prophecies such as those in Daniel and Revelation must apply to Israel and only to Israel.

11

INTERPRETING END-TIMES PASSAGES

If biblical passages can have more than one application, how are we to interpret the Bible's end-times texts? Let's first review the four traditional ways of interpreting this literature, using the book of Revelation as an example.

1. The *preterist* interpretation holds that Revelation describes events in the first century and that the beast of chapter 13 is the Roman Empire and/or its Caesars. Those who agree with this view see little or no future reference in Revelation.

2. The *historicist* interpretation holds that Revelation describes events throughout history. Jonathon Edwards believed that the fifth bowl of divine wrath mentioned in Rev. 16:10-11 was the Reformation. This illustrates the historicist position: specific events throughout history have been foretold. Many of these lie in the past; some are still to come.

3. The *futurist* interpretation holds that most of Revelation (especially after chap. 3) is about the end of history. Dispensationalists accept the futurist view.

4. The *idealist* interpretation holds that Revelation is not about events of the past or future. Instead, it symbolizes the salvation of the soul and the struggle between God's kingdom and evil.

The preterist, historicist, and futurist views have one common fault. They all assume that any given prophecy has one and only one fulfillment. The only thing that distinguishes these views from one another is whether they hold the prophecies were fulfilled in the first century (preterism), over the course of many centuries (historicism), or still lie in the future (futurism). But there is no reason to assume that prophetic texts have only one fulfillment. As we observed earlier, the Bible itself shows us that scripture passages can have more than one application. The same is true for prophecies; they can have more than one fulfillment. In fact, instead of thinking about prophecies being fulfilled, or "filled full," it is better to think of these texts as having multiple applications in history. Their significance is not limited to a single fulfillment.

We've already seen the way in which Hos. 11:1 ("out of Egypt I called my son") has a double reference. For Hosea, it pointed backward to Israel's redemption from bondage in Egypt. For Matthew it pointed forward to Jesus Christ. With this example in mind we can look at some other prophecies and see that they can apply to multiple points in history.

Take, for instance, Amos 9:11-12: "On that day I will raise up the booth of David that is fallen, and repair its breaches. . . . that they may possess . . . all the nations." Like many Old Testament prophecies, this relates to the restoration of Israel after Babylonian exile. The prophets anticipated that God would renew Israel's national existence and provide a king like David (see Isa. 11:1-5 for another expression of the same hope). In Acts, however, Amos's prophecy is interpreted to mean that God would gather Gentiles into the church (Acts 15:13-17). At one level, Amos's words applied to Israel's national history—Israel was indeed restored after the Babylonian exile. At another level, his words applied to the church as Gentiles came to be incorporated into the people of God through the apostles' preaching. This example shows us clearly that prophetic passages can have more than one application or significance.

Or take Joel 2:28-32: "I will pour out my spirit on all flesh; your sons and your daughters shall prophesy . . ." For Joel, these words referred to the end of history, when God would do great wonders to redeem Israel and create a new order. Acts, however, sees Joel's prophecy as being significant for the days of the apostles (Acts 2:16-21). Now, no one thinks that Joel's prophecy was *completely* fulfilled in Acts 2; the Spirit was not poured out on literally *all* flesh. The Holiness Movement, for example, has taught that in the future God would again pour out the Spirit in a dramatic and even more universal way.[13] So we should think of Acts 2 as being a preliminary and partial application of Joel's prophecy, with other applications still in the future.

These examples show us that prophecies are typically not fulfilled by a single historical event. Prophetic words do not describe single moments in history. Instead, they describe patterns of God's activity—ways in which God acts repeatedly in history. That is why New Testament writers could see that prophecies about Israel's restoration apply also to Jesus.

Since most prophecies are not "filled full" by only one event or moment in history, their complete fulfillment is yet to come. For instance, Zechariah's prophecy, "Your king comes to you; triumphant and victorious is he, humble and riding on a donkey" (Zech. 9:9) was partially fulfilled when Jesus entered Jerusalem (Matt. 21:1-5); however, no one imagines that this event was a complete fulfillment. Jesus' first appearance introduced the kingdom of God into history with great power. But the kingdom still must strive with the powers of sin and darkness; its victory is not complete. The complete filling-full of the prophet's words will come only in Christ's final triumph at the end of history. Only then will such prophetic hopes find a total realization. Only then will the messianic age, with its blessings and complete victory over sin, be fully actualized. Only Christ's return in glory will fully fill the Old Testament's messianic promises.

12

HONORING THE
ORIGINAL SETTING

The fact that prophetic texts are normally filled full in stages and have multiple applications helps us interpret these texts in a responsible way. What this means is that if we focus only on their final fulfillment in the second coming of Jesus (as end-times specialists tend to do), then we overlook other important layers of meaning.

Take the book of Revelation as an example. It is common for Christians to interpret this book (or at least chaps. 4–22) as pertaining strictly to the future—*our* future. And it is appropriate for us to interpret Revelation as speaking to us and our future. But we don't get the full impact of Revelation unless we hear its message for its first-century readers and hearers. It's important to remember that Revelation is above all a letter to seven churches. These churches, at the end of the first century, had some problems, and Revelation addresses those problems. The chief issue for Revelation is the churches' need to remain faithful to God and to resist compromise with the Roman Empire. *Responsible interpretation has to honor Revelation's original purpose.* It's important to see that Revelation is speaking to first-century Christians about first-century concerns.

This means that when we read about the beast that rises from the sea (13:1) and the other beast from the land (13:11) and the great prostitute (chap. 17), we should ask, "What was the message for the seven churches?" It is critically important to keep in mind the following point: If Revelation was to truly be a word of warning and encouragement to the seven churches, the message of Revelation had to make sense to its first readers. It had to be addressing matters of concern to them. So how would the first-century readers understand the symbols of the beast from the sea and beast from the land and the great prostitute? They would understand them as symbols of the Roman Empire.

How do we know that first-century readers would interpret Revelation's symbols as a description of the Roman Empire? There are two reasons. First, a general consideration: If Revelation was to function as a message of warning and encouragement to the seven churches, then it must have spoken of realities that were threatening them. Revelation wouldn't be a very effective warning or encouragement for its first readers if it referred to events thousands of years in their future. Second, consider the message of the book.

- In chapter 3 Jesus promises to keep the Philadelphians "from the hour of trial that is coming on the whole world" (v. 10). This tells us that persecution was on the readers' immediate horizon. The source of this persecution could only be the Roman Empire; it was the only thing in the first century capable of creating a worldwide "trial."
- In chapter 13 Revelation speaks of a beast with seven heads. We learn in 17:9-11 that the heads

represent seven kings, with the beast being an eighth king. First-century readers would have understood the heads as symbols for the list of Roman emperors.

- According to 13:3, one of the heads had been apparently killed but then revived. First-century readers would have seen this as a reference to the Emperor Nero, who had been assassinated; however, there were persistent rumors that Nero had actually survived and fled to safety.

- According to 17:8, the beast "was, and is not, and is about to ascend from the bottomless pit." This is another way of referring to Nero, who "was" (i.e., was alive until assassinated), and "is not" (i.e., was dead when Revelation was written), and "is about to ascend" (i.e., would return). Ancient sources tells us there was a widespread belief that Nero would return to Rome at the head of an army.[14]

- The enemy of God's people is referred to as "Babylon the great" (17:5). Jewish literature around the time of Jesus frequently referred to Rome as Babylon.

- In 13:11-15 the beast is depicted as the object of worship. First-century Christians would interpret this as a reference to the worship given to the Roman emperors.

- The seven heads are identified as seven mountains (17:9); and the prostitute who rides the beast symbolizes "the great city that rules over the kings of the earth" (v. 18). First-century readers would have easily seen these images to be references to Rome.

- The beast has a number, 666. When these numbers are interpreted as letters (ancient languages used the same symbols for letters and numbers), they spell various names, including "Nero."

To sum up: responsible interpretation honors the original setting of a book like Revelation. In its original setting, Revelation spoke a word of warning and encouragement in the context of the Roman Empire and the threat of persecution. The first readers of Revelation received it as a prophetic word because it spoke of matters that concerned them deeply and addressed issues they faced every day. Revelation for them was not a book of mysteries. Even the number 666 could be understood—that is why Revelation urged its readers to use wisdom and to understand the reference (13:18). Revelation expected its readers to understand its symbols. But they could understand them only because the symbols stood for realities the readers experienced every day.

13

APPLYING BIBLICAL TEXTS

The first-century meaning of Revelation does not exhaust Revelation's message. As we observed earlier, prophetic books can be applied more than once. Revelation speaks as powerfully today as it did in the first century. However, before we can think about its meaning for today, we need to examine some common presuppositions that get in the way of responsible interpretation.

People often get puzzled about how a book like Revelation can be applied at various times in history. The puzzlement rests on the assumption that Revelation describes a future that is fixed. It's as though history were a film whose script were written in advance. In filmmaking, the script is written first. Then the director and actors perform the script. Many people think of history in this way. God has written a script. It specifies exactly what will happen in history and when it will happen. Each line in the script describes one and only one historical event. History happens as humans perform their scripted roles. In this view, Revelation and other prophetic books are a portion of the script we've been allowed to read. Reading these books is like reading a film's script before the actors perform it. Once we read the script, we know just what the actors will do.

To change the metaphor, many people think of history as a huge calendar. On this calendar God long ago filled in events on every date. For example, in the beginning God decreed this author's birth in 1956 and filled in the event on the big cosmic calendar. For the year AD 70 God decreed the destruction of Jerusalem by the Romans and placed those events on the calendar. In the same way, God has decreed all the events of the future, including end-times events. Each event will happen when its day on the calendar comes around. The book of Revelation describes those future events and provides some details about the calendar. Those who study carefully can, it is thought, figure out parts of the calendar and thus know when the end-times events will happen.

There is one big problem with viewing history as a script and a calendar—these metaphors flatly contradict what the Bible says about history. These metaphors treat history as a collection of events, the details of which God has determined from the beginning. They assume that before creating the universe, God decided (like a scriptwriter) exactly what would happen and how and when it would happen. Thus God has predetermined all the details of the universe's history. Although Christians believe that God has *plans* for the universe and that God will someday fully realize the kingdom of God, believing that God predetermines the details of the universe's history means God is the real author and cause of evil. This conclusion is intolerable for Christians. Fortunately, the prophetic literature of the Bible presents God and history very differently.

Take, for example, the book of Jonah. God commissions Jonah to declare that "forty days more, and Nineveh shall be overthrown" (Jonah 3:4). However, the Ninevites unexpectedly repented. Did God go forward with the destruction of Nineveh? Was this destruction already part of an unchangeable script? Was it already entered onto the cosmic calendar? Was God bound to destroy Nineveh in spite of their repentance? No. On the contrary, the course of Nineveh's history changed because of their actions. This tells us that history is not locked into place. It is not a preordained script or calendar. Instead, history is shaped and changed according to what human beings do.

Of course, the story of Jonah does not imply that history is simply the sum total of human actions. On the contrary, God is the principal actor in history, and God's actions give meaning to the story and establish the overall direction the story takes. But God does not act alone. God interacts with human actors, like the people of Nineveh. As human actors act, God works in and through their actions to lead history toward its goal.

In the book of Jeremiah, this belief is stated clearly. Using the example of a potter who reworks a lump of clay into a new vessel, the word of the Lord came to Jeremiah:

> I may declare concerning a nation or a kingdom, that I will pluck up and break down and destroy it, but if that nation . . . turns from its evil, I will change my mind about the disaster that I intended to bring on it. (Jer. 18:7-8)

This passage directly states that the future, including Israel's future, is not scripted in advance. It shows us that, although God's overall plan to redeem humankind is constant and unchanging, God's interaction with human actors is flexible and responsive.

Accordingly, there is no reason to assume that Revelation describes events that are already scripted. They are not already entered onto God's calendar, each with an assigned and unchangeable date. Instead, we should think of Revelation as describing a recurrent pattern in history, a repeating pattern of fulfillment. In this pattern, God's people find themselves threatened by a hostile cultural and political system. This system demands everyone's allegiance and makes itself an object of worship. In this situation, God's people are faced with an either-or choice. They must choose to worship God alone or to compromise with the political system. The book of Revelation speaks powerfully to Christians of every century because it describes a pattern that happens repeatedly in human history. The words of Revelation were thus fulfilled in the first century, when Christians waged spiritual warfare against the Roman Empire. But Christians in later centuries experienced Revelation as a living word to them because they too found themselves under demonic political structures. So we can speak of Revelation finding further fulfillment in later centuries. Since we can be sure Christians will suffer under demonic political structures in the future, we know that Revelation does describe the future. But it doesn't describe only the future. It describes every situation in history when God's people are threatened by a demonic political system.

This means that the revivalistic eschatology of Jonathon Edwards and Charles Finney was correct—human action does influence the coming of the kingdom of God. The spread or hindrance of revival does affect the timing of that coming. It also means that much end-times theology is wrong. This is because it assumes that the future is already scripted: on such and such a date the rapture will occur, on such and such a date the Antichrist will appear, on such and such a date the two witnesses of Rev. 11 will be killed, and so on. Most end-times theology assumes these and all other end-times events are entered onto God's calendar. Each day brings us closer to those events. But from the perspective of Jonah and Jeremiah, this way of thinking is greatly mistaken.

We interpret the book of Revelation and other prophetic texts appropriately when (1) we honor their original setting, (2) we read them according to their purpose of providing warning and encouragement, and (3) apply their purpose to our own day. For example, we apply the book of Revelation to our own day by using it to help us discern demonic political powers today. As we read Revelation, we should ask, "In what ways have we compromised the worship of God alone? In what ways have we cooperated with demonic political systems in our day?" These are the questions that agree with Revelation's purpose for us.

CONCLUSION
TOP MISTAKES MADE ABOUT
THE END TIMES

As a conclusion let's look at some of the biggest mistakes that are often made about the end times. Although we have already discussed many of these errors, this section will serve as a summary and a reminder of the importance of careful biblical interpretation.

Dispensationalism's View of Israel and the Church

Of all the mistakes made by end-times specialists, this is the most unusual. This view holds that Israel, not the church, is the true focus of God's purposes in history. As a result, dispensationalists believe the church age is an interruption of God's historical plan. It's difficult to see how any serious student of the New Testament could accept this view.

The Idea of the Rapture

For dispensationalists, in order for God to get the attention back on Israel, it is necessary to remove the church from the world. This is why they believe in the idea of the rapture. As should be clear by now, the only reason for believing in the rapture is because it is required by dispensationalism's view of the church and Israel. There is no support in the New Testament for this idea. But what about 1 Thess. 4:17 ("Then we who are alive . . . will be caught up in the clouds")? Doesn't that describe the rapture of the church? No, it doesn't. Biblical scholars have shown that Paul here was referring, not to the rapture, but to something quite different. In the ancient world, when a great ruler would make an official visit to a city, such a visit was known as a "parousia." As the ruler approached the city, leading members of the city would go out to greet him and to escort him into the city. This is what Paul was describing. Jesus will return to the earth as a great king. This return will be a parousia: "For this we declare to you by the word of the Lord, that we who are alive, who are left until the coming [parousia] of the Lord, will by no means precede those who have died" (v. 15). The church will ascend to the clouds to meet Jesus and escort him to earth, so that he can begin ruling. First Thessalonians 4:17 is not about the church leaving the world; it is about the church meeting Jesus and joining him as he triumphantly comes to earth.

Signs of the Times

According to many end-times theologians, we know we are near the end times because all of the signs Jesus mentioned—war, famine, natural disasters, and so on—are taking place daily. The problem here is that these realities have been found in every century. Are there really more natural disasters today than in the year 1000? Or 1500? Or 1900? More war today than in earlier centuries? What is at work here is the common human tendency to think our time is the worst of all—that things are much worse today than they have ever been. There is really no evidence supporting this belief.

Indirect Date Setting

Mindful of Jesus' words that not even the Son of Man knows the hour and day of his return, end-times specialists repeatedly tell us they are not setting dates for Christ's return. But they continually drop hints that the end is near and provide signs-of-the-times count-downs to the tribulation. Their real message is that the end times are very near. But as anyone who has studied history knows, almost every century has seen its share of date setters. There is nothing wrong with setting dates for Christ's return, but this activity continually proves to be a fruitless endeavor.

Apostasy of the Church

End-times theologians often believe that the church today has fallen into widespread apostasy. They hold this view because of their conviction that during the end times the majority of the church will fall away from God. Many end-times writers actually believe that only a small portion of the church is authentically Christian. This is part of their signs-of-the-times theol-ogy: Everything, including the church, is much worse today than it has ever been. In reality, the church has had good days and bad days. It will always have good days and bad days. Today there are places where the church is strong and places where it is weak. It will al-ways be so. But it is incorrect to believe that the church today is largely a picture of apostasy.

The Interpretation of Days and Weeks in Daniel

End-times specialists frequently state that the "days" and "weeks" in Daniel (for example, the 2,300 days of chap. 8 or the seventy weeks of chap. 9) really refer to years. They base this on the assumption that in prophetic literature each day represents a year. As a rule of interpretation, this is a highly questionable assumption. Besides, proponents of this view never apply this day = year assumption to Revelation; doing so would be unreasonable. But this inconsistency is a minor problem compared to the fact that their day = year assumption produces calculations that contradict their conclusions. Their calculations force them to maintain there is a more than two thousand-year gap between the sixty-ninth and seventieth "week" of Daniel's prophecy. The sixty-ninth week corresponds to Jesus' ministry. The seventieth week corresponds to the great tribulation. So there is a gap between these "weeks." This gap is needed to make sense of the theory. It has no basis in the book of Daniel. Along with this gap idea is another problem—that in prophecy a year really consists of 360 days. This assumption is necessary to make the calculations agree with real history. But this again is just a way to maintain the theory. It has no basis in accepted biblical studies.

Not Acknowledging Error

When it comes to interpreting the Bible, no one bats one thousand. However, it's one thing to be wrong; it's another not to acknowledge you are wrong. Take the Adventist groups that followed William Miller and experienced the Great Disappointment. You might imagine that they finally admitted their error. After all, Jesus did not return in 1844. However, they made no such admission. Instead, they continued to assert that Jesus had returned, in a sense, in 1844. But he hadn't returned to earth. Instead, he moved from one part of the heavenly temple to another, in preparation for his return to earth. Likewise, the Jehovah's Witnesses predicted Jesus would return in 1914. When 1914 came and went, they didn't admit their error. They simply argued that Jesus had returned and that he did so secretly and invisibly.

Misinterpreting Revelation

No one claims that the book of Revelation is easy to interpret. However, end-times specialists tend to interpret Revelation in a very rigid way. For example, Revelation portrays three sets of disasters resulting from three events: the opening of the seals on the scroll (Rev. 6–8), the angels' blowing their trumpets (chaps. 8–11), and the angels pouring out bowls full of God's wrath (chap. 16). Different persons have spent much effort over the years trying to relate all these disasters to history. The assumption is often that the disasters of the seals will come (or has come) first, followed by the disasters of the trumpets, and finally will come the disasters of the bowls. But this assumption presupposes that Revelation presents us with a narrative of events that can be arranged in chronological order. This assumption overlooks the fact that Revelation is not really a narrative. It is instead a book of symbols. It is thus a mistake to try to discern a chronology from the book of Revelation.

Untenable Interpretations of Political History

End-times specialists convinced themselves in the 1970s that the Soviet Union would one day lead the Arab world in an invasion of Israel. The collapse of the Soviet Union and the declining power of Russia have not resulted in a change of view. We still find end-times experts proclaiming a future invasion by Russia. There are several problems with this idea. First, there is no biblical support for it. Second, it overlooks the fact that Egypt and Jordan have had official diplomatic, peaceful relations with Israel for many years and that, except for Iran, Israel's other neighbors show no interest in war. Israel's political troubles relate to its treatment of the Palestinian people (some of whom are Christians); there are no hostile political relations between Israel and its political neighbors. The beliefs of the end-times experts are, accordingly, without basis.

Overconfidence

Perhaps the biggest mistake of end-times theologians is their persistent belief that they have discovered the key to biblical interpretation. While it is a good thing to stand by one's convictions, it is not good to be too overly confident. A person must continually expand his or her perspective and explore other possibilities. Resting too firmly on just one viewpoint can lead to repeated errors, which has often been the case with speculation about the end times.

✳ ✳ ✳

Christians have been thinking about the Bible for two thousand years. We need to listen to other voices and learn from them. We need a generous approach to the Bible, with more emphasis on the prophetic purpose of warning and encouragement and less attention on unlocking secrets and deciphering codes. In short, we should read the Bible, not so much to satisfy our curiosity, but rather to be trained in righteousness.

NOTES

1. "CNN/Time Poll conducted by Harris Interactive" (June 19-20, 2002), Religion, PollingReport.com, http://www.pollingreport.com/religion3.htm (accessed January 17, 2011).

2. "A Lutheran Response to the 'Left Behind' Series," A Report of the Commission on Theology and Church Relations of The Lutheran Church–Missouri Synod (2004), 6-9, http://www.lcms.org/graphics/assets/media/CTCR/LeftBehind.pdf (accessed June 21, 2010).

3. Stephen Travis, "Has Real Hope Been 'Left Behind'?" Methodist Evangelicals Together, http://www.met-uk.org/met/article.php?cat=general&id=166&PHPSESSID=8ad757ca16cf2787c16b37cc03b3b1ce (accessed June 21, 2010).

4. Dallas Theological Seminary's statement on dispensations and the pre-tribulation rapture can be found here: "DTS Doctrinal Statement," DTS Web site, http://www.dts.edu/about/doctrinal-statement/; Moody's eschatology can be found here: "The Second Coming of Christ," Moody Bible Institute, http://www.moodyministries.net/crp_MainPage.aspx?id=644 (accessed June 23, 2010).

5. "Preamble and Articles of Faith," Church of the Nazarene, http://www.nazarene.org/ministries/administration/visitorcenter/articles/display.aspx (accessed November 18, 2010).

6. "Our 16 Fundamental Truths," General Council of the Assemblies of God, http://ag.org/top/beliefs/statement_of_fundamental_truths/sft_full.cfm (accessed November 18, 2010).

7. "Many Americans Uneasy with Mix of Religion and Politics," The Pew Forum on Religion and Public Life, http://pewforum.org/Politics-and-Elections/Many-Americans-Uneasy-with-Mix-of-Religion-and-Politics.aspx (accessed November 18, 2010).

8. *Merriam-Webster's Collegiate Dictionary*, s.v. "hermeneutic," http://unabridged.merriam-webster.com (accessed November 30, 2010).

9. Lawrence Wright, "Forcing the End," Public Broadcasting Service, http://www.pbs.org/wgbh/pages/frontline/shows/apocalypse/readings/forcing.html (accessed June 23, 2010).

10. "Signs in the Sun, Moon, and Stars," Jack Van Impe Ministries International, http://www.jvim.com/ib/2009/11/sunmoon.html (accessed June 23, 2010).

11. "Pre-Trib Perspectives," Tim LaHaye Ministries, https://timlahaye.com/shopcontent.asp?type=PreTribResearch (accessed June 24, 2010).

12. Earl Radmacher, "The Nature and Result of Literal Interpretation," Pre-Trib Research Center, http://www.pre-trib.org/articles/view/nature-and-result-of-literal-interpretation (accessed June 24, 2010).

13. Melvin E. Dieter, "The Development of Holiness Theology in Nineteenth Century America," *Wesleyan Theological* Journal 20, no. 1 (1985): 72-73; Melvin E. Dieter, *The Holiness Revival of the Nineteenth Century* (Metuchen, N.J.: The Scarecrow Press, 1980), 5.

14. Suetonius says that some astrologers had predicted Nero would be overthrown but then restored to power (*Life of Nero*, 40.2). Tacitus reports that after Nero's death some believed he was still alive (*Histories*, 2.8). Suetonius and Tacitus also tell us that in the years following Nero's death, several people appeared claiming to be Nero.

GLOSSARY

Apocalypse: The Greek word for revelation.

Apocalyptic: A type of literature that emphasizes resurrection, judgment, end-time disasters, and other eschatological phenomena.

Chiliasm (an approximate pronunciation in English would be "kill-i-asm"): The idea that Christ's millennial rule (mentioned in Revelation) will be a literal thousand-year period.

Dispensationalism: A way of interpreting the Bible. It focuses on the difference between God's will for Israel and God's will for the church and teaches that the Old Testament's end-times prophecies all apply to Israel and not the church.

Eschatology: The doctrine of history's end and related events, such as resurrection and judgment.

Hermeneutics: The process of interpretation. Interpreting the Bible is an exercise in hermeneutics.

Kingdom of God: The rule of God. According to the Gospels, this was the focus of Jesus' teaching.

Millennium: The thousand-year rule of Jesus, mentioned in Rev. 20.

Parousia: The return of Jesus to the world.

Rapture: The dispensationalist idea that God will, at some future point, remove all Christians from the world and take them to heaven.

Tribulation: The period (according to dispensationalist theology) of disasters and trauma just before the return of Christ to the world.

BIBLIOGRAPHY

Dunning, H. Ray. *Grace, Faith, and Holiness: A Wesleyan Systematic Theology*. Kansas City: Beacon Hill Press of Kansas City, 1988.

Dunning, H. Ray, ed. *The Second Coming: A Wesleyan Approach to the Doctrine of Last Things*. Kansas City: Beacon Hill Press of Kansas City, 1995.

Powell, Samuel M. *Discovering Our Christian Faith*. Kansas City: Beacon Hill Press of Kansas City, 2008.